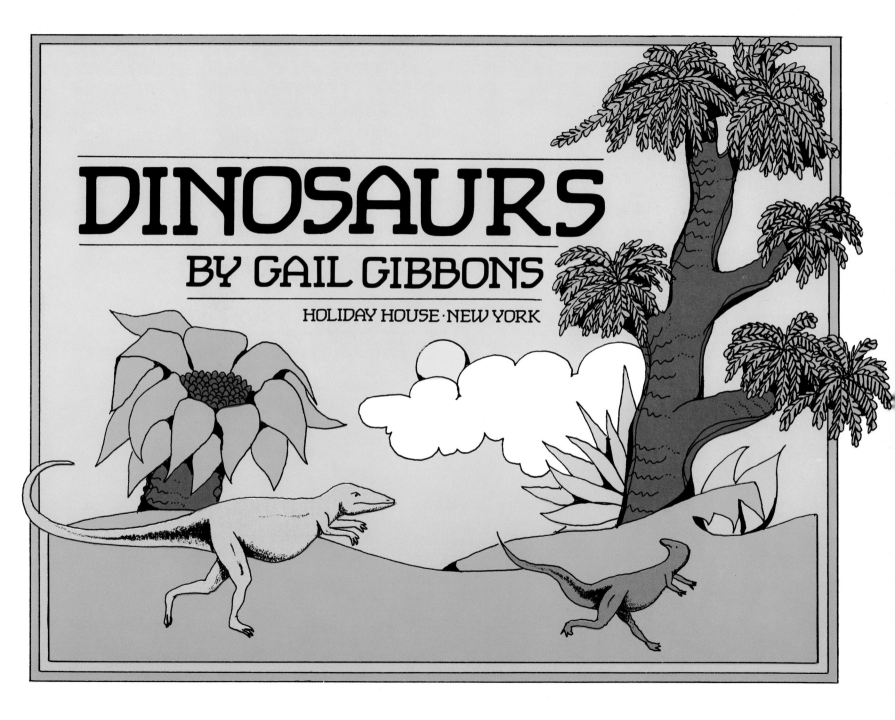

DINOSAURS

BY GAIL GIBBONS

HOLIDAY HOUSE · NEW YORK

For dinosaur fan, David Rogers

Special thanks to The American Museum of
Natural History, New York City

Copyright © 1987 by Gail Gibbons
All rights reserved
Printed in the United States of America

Library of Congress Cataloging-in-Publication Data

Gibbons, Gail.
Dinosaurs.

Summary: Introduces in simple text and illustrations
the characteristics and habits of a variety of
dinosaurs.
1. Dinosaurs—Juvenile literature. [1. Dinosaurs]
I. Title.
QE862.D5G345 1987   567.9′1   87-364
ISBN 0-8234-0657-1
ISBN 0-8234-0708-x (pbk.)

Dinosaurs lived long, long ago, even before people lived on earth. They ruled and roamed the land for millions of years.

Some were small . . .

others were big . . .

and some were huge.

Today, there aren't any living dinosaurs.
They died about 70 million years ago.
When they died, sand and mud covered their
bodies. Millions of years went by and the
mud and sand turned into stone. The dinosaur
bones became fossils.

A fossil is the
hardened remains
or traces of plant
or animal life in
rock.

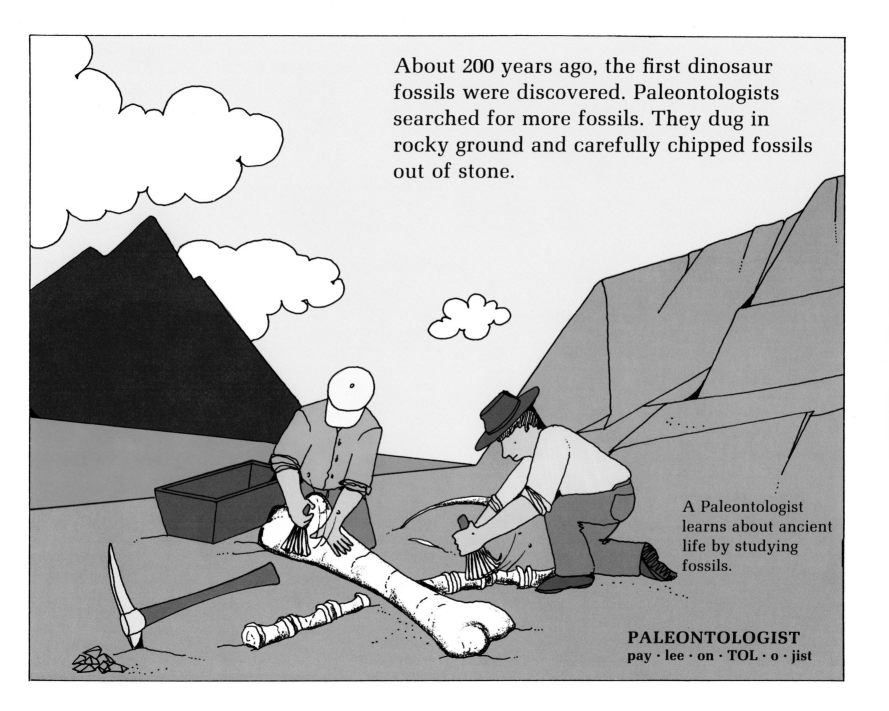

About 200 years ago, the first dinosaur fossils were discovered. Paleontologists searched for more fossils. They dug in rocky ground and carefully chipped fossils out of stone.

A Paleontologist learns about ancient life by studying fossils.

PALEONTOLOGIST
pay · lee · on · TOL · o · jist

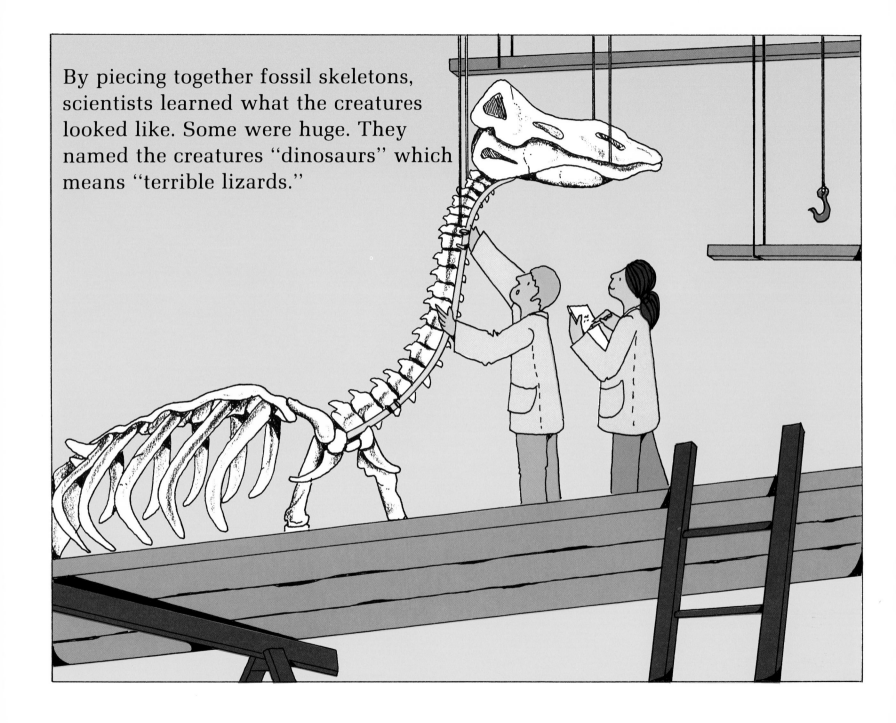

By piecing together fossil skeletons, scientists learned what the creatures looked like. Some were huge. They named the creatures "dinosaurs" which means "terrible lizards."

Paleontologists have also learned how dinosaurs lived by studying their remains. They have discovered that not all dinosaurs were terrible. Some were peaceful.

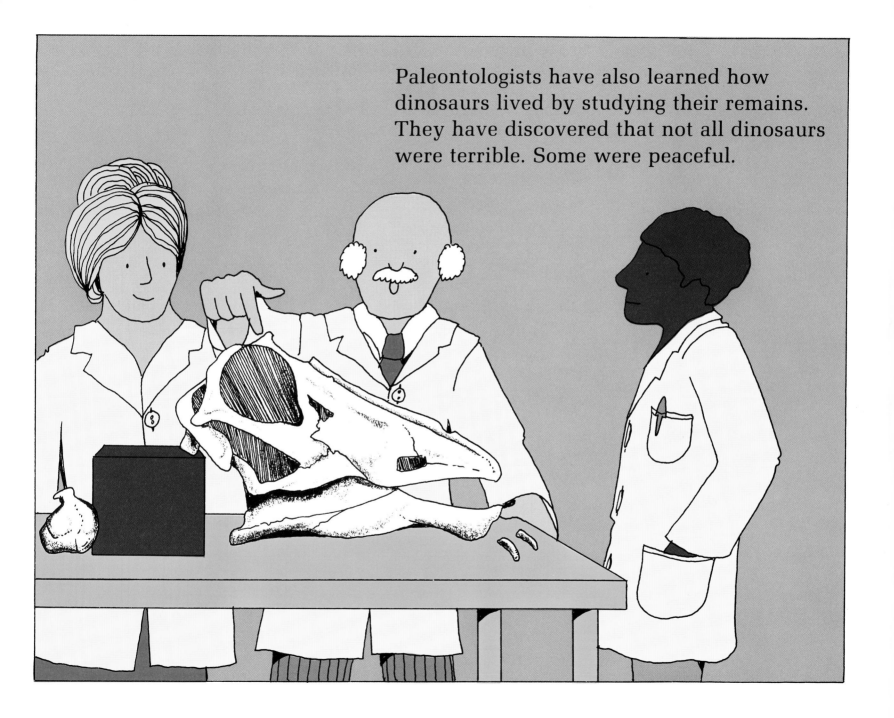

Ankylosaurus was a plant eater. Spikes and plates were all over its body. Its tail was used for protection against meat-eating dinosaurs.

ANKYLOSAURUS
an · KILE · o · sore · us

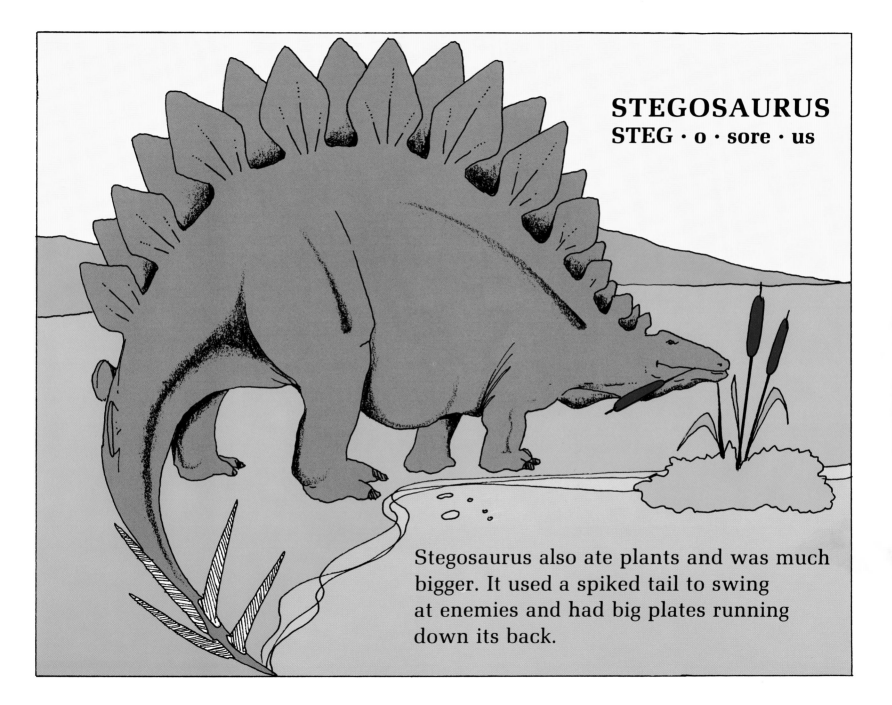

STEGOSAURUS
STEG · o · sore · us

Stegosaurus also ate plants and was much bigger. It used a spiked tail to swing at enemies and had big plates running down its back.

Protoceratops and Triceratops ate plants, too.

PROTOCERATOPS
pro · toe · SARE · a · tops

They had big heads with shields to protect their necks from sharp teeth. They were about 20 feet long.

TRICERATOPS
try · SARE · a · tops

Iguanodon stood up on its strong back legs and used its spiked thumbs for protection. Iguanodon used its many teeth to crush and chop plants.

IGUANODON
ig · WAN · o · don

Anatosaurus used its duckbill to get water plants from swamp bottoms. It was about 14 feet tall and 35 feet long.

ANATOSAURUS
ah · NAT · o · sore · us

One huge creature was Apatosaurus. It weighed as much as six elephants. Apatosaurus used its long neck to reach down under water for plants.

APATOSAURUS
ah · PAT · o · sore · us

sometimes called

Brontosaurus
BRON · toe · sore · us

One of the very biggest of all dinosaurs was Brachiosaurus. It stood about 40 feet tall and was 80 feet long. Brachiosaurus liked eating water plants, too.

BRACHIOSAURUS
BRAK · e · o · sore · us

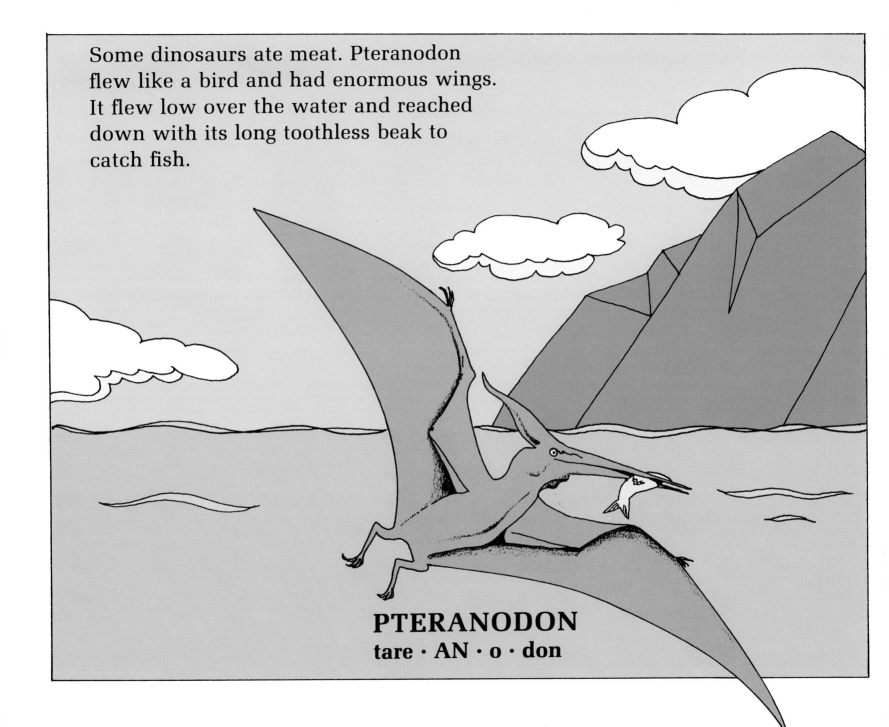

Some dinosaurs ate meat. Pteranodon flew like a bird and had enormous wings. It flew low over the water and reached down with its long toothless beak to catch fish.

PTERANODON
tare · AN · o · don

ELASMOSAURUS
el · AZ · mo · sore · us

Another fish-eater was Elasmosaurus. It
lived in water and used its fins as oars.
Elasmosaurus had long, sharp teeth.

Coelurosaurus was a small dinosaur.
It was able to run very fast to catch
small animals and to get away from
the bigger dinosaurs.

COELUROSAURUS
see · LUR · o · sore · us

ORNITHOLESTES
or · nith · o · LESS · teez

Ornitholestes was small, too. It was a swift hunter and ate any creature it could catch that was smaller than itself.

Some dinosaurs really were terrible.
Allosaurus was very big and had a huge
mouth full of sharp teeth.

ALLOSAURUS
AL · o · sore · us

Allosaurus even ate big dinosaurs like Apatosaurus.

Tyrannosaurus rex was the scariest of them all. It was king of the dinosaurs and was the most terrible animal that ever roamed the earth. Tyrannosaurus rex stood about 20 feet tall and had teeth six inches long.

TYRANNOSAURUS REX
tih · RAN · o · sore · us rex

All dinosaurs,
big and small,
were terrified of
Tyrannosaurus rex.

Dinosaurs lived on earth for 140 million years. Paleontologists know that millions of years ago something happened that killed these animals.

One theory is that our planet became very hot and the dinosaurs died from the heat.

A recent theory is that a meteor hit
the earth, throwing dust into the air.
The sun couldn't shine through the
dust to keep plant life alive. The
planet became too cold for the dinosaurs
to live.

Paleontologists are always learning more about dinosaurs. They were amazing creatures, large and small.

DINOSAUR FOOTPRINTS

Millions of years ago dinosaurs walked the earth. Sometimes they left footprints in soft mud. The mud hardened. Over millions of years, the mud footprints turned to fossils.

Some are huge.

Some are small.

The biggest fossil footprint that has been found is 2½ feet long. It was made by Apatosaurus.

They don't all look the same.

Facts Learned From Footprints

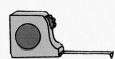 Paleontologists can learn what kind of dinosaur made a footprint.

They can figure out how big the dinosaur was.

 They learn which dinosaurs walked on their hind feet.

 When they find many of the same kind of tracks in one area, they know that these dionsaurs traveled in herds.

If smaller tracks are found inside a herd, they know these dinosaurs protected their young.

If they find a dinosaur footprint with webbed feet, they learn that it is possible that the area might have been near a body of water at one time . . . millions and millions of years ago.